WAYS TO CONQUER ADDICTION: A GUIDE TO RETURNING TO YOUR NORMAL LIFE.

DANIEL C. NUNN.

TABLE OF CONTENT

Chapter 1

What is ADDICTION?

What is addiction?

Addiction is an inability to quit taking a drug or participating in a habit even while it is inflicting psychological and bodily damage.

The word addiction does not simply relate to dependency on narcotics such as heroin or cocaine. Some addictions also entail an inability to cease indulging in activities such as gambling, eating, sex, or working.

Chapter 2

OVERVIEW ABOUT ADDICTION.

A lifestyle issue. Understanding the etiology of drug use is crucial as this may allow the identification of possible areas of difficulty in functioning which may consequently act as target areas for appropriate treatment and intervention [1]. However, for even the most experienced physicians, it may often be difficult to recognize and understand the various underlying variables that could drive an individual's drug use and how these factors may be interrelated.

Further complicating things is that there may be substantial, sometimes causative links between each of the contributing elements behind drug use, including mental health and social functioning challenges, relationship problems, and other stressful life conditions [2]. There are also multiple ways in which substance use is referred to in the literature, with several distinct diagnostic categories describing different kinds of substance use and differing degrees of severity of dependence [3], leading some researchers to refer to the broader, general category of 'substance use disorders (SUD) (e.g.[4]) (e.g.[4]). For brevity throughout this essay, SUD will be used to refer to the vast variety of kinds of drug use.

Exploration and comprehension of the causal linkages between each of these areas of difficulty provide a crucial initial step in the therapy process [5]. This may be especially significant for persons who are 'dually diagnosed', i.e. are having comorbid mental health challenges such as depression and anxiety with their SUD, since sometimes mental health difficulties may be causally associated with SUD [6]. The literature demonstrates that many individuals, as much as 75 – 85% of the substance-using population, may self-medicate with substances in an attempt to alleviate mental health difficulties [7], although for many their use of substances may exacerbate the severity of their mental health difficulties.

*People grow hooked on various things:
Tangible eg\sDrugs \sperson etc.
Intangible eg\sGambling\sgame\sSex etc.

NOTE: Addiction is distinct from dedication (Addiction reduces you while devotion boosts you.

*Coping skills vs escape routes: Coping skills are Price people pay in other to be able to overcome certain challenges in life or what is confronting them that are inborn while escape routes are alternative partway through which people try to solve what is challenging them rather than facing there fears squarely, escape routes are never a solution but a manipulation to the solution that never last. Eg, suppose a guy that becomes drunk in other to forget his issue as an escape route, when the drunkenness is cleaned up by the break of day, he still has his problem to confront.

Chapter 3

FACTOR THAT ENHANCES ADDICTION.

- Genetic (40-60%)

+Chronic stress

Stress has long been recognized to enhance sensitivity to addiction. The past decade has led to a tremendous gain in understanding of the underlying processes driving this connection. Behavioral and neurological correlations are being uncovered, and some evidence of molecular and cellular alterations related to chronic stress and addiction has been identified. Human research has benefitted from the introduction of powerful brain-imaging technologies and the cross investigation of laboratory-induced ways of stress and desire and their relationship to particular brain areas involved with reward and addiction risk. This research focuses mostly on the link between stress and addiction in humans but also pulls from the larger animal literature to support the stated assumptions. A description of stress and its brain roots is offered with special attention to its impact on motivation and behavior. Against the backdrop of the considerable epidemiological evidence relating to early childhood and adult adversity and the risk of addiction, discoveries from fundamental and human research that indicate possible processes underlying this connection are discussed. A crucial role is identified for prefrontal circuits involved in adaptive learning and executive function, particularly managing discomfort and desires/impulses, in the link between stress and addiction risk. However, some concerns remain unsolved in understanding stress-related addiction risk, and they are examined to influence future studies. Finally, the consequences of chronic drug use on stress and reward circuits specifically concerning relapse risk are investigated. Prospects in treating stress-related relapse risk in clinical settings are also highlighted.

- Social pressure

Friends and other peers may have an increasingly powerful impact throughout the adolescent years. Teens who use drugs may persuade even those without risk factors to try drugs for the first time. Teens are confronted with peer pressure and might easily be tempted to experiment with drugs to fit in.

- Adverse childhood experience

Adverse childhood experiences (ACEs) are commonly characterized as stressful and/or traumatic situations that occur throughout childhood (1, 2). (1, 2). Research had indicated that more than 60% of adults report having at least one unpleasant childhood event, and 17% have four or more unfavorable childhood experiences (3). (3). There is emerging evidence that persons with ACEs are at increased risk for illnesses (e.g., alcoholism, myocardial infarction, stroke, depression, diabetes, and coronary heart disease) and disability related to health status (4–8). (4–8). Moreover, ACEs are a key risk factor for drug misuse. For instance, childhood maltreatment is highly connected to marijuana usage (9, 10). (9, 10). Individuals with ACE scores ≥ 5 are seven to 10 times more likely to report illicit drug addiction compared to those without ACEs (11) and are four to 12 times more likely to become drug abusers. In summary, ACEs not only impact physical and mental health but also raise the chance of drug misuse in adulthood.

Depression is one of the most prevalent and major unpleasant feelings generated by ACEs. Compared with other unpleasant emotions, the influence of sadness on drug addiction has more essential clinical importance. Many studies have found an association between ACEs and depression, as individuals with ACEs are more likely to suffer from depression compared to those without such experiences. Emotional, sexual, and physical child maltreatment is the most prominent danger factor for depression. A retrospective cohort research demonstrated that the risk of depressive illnesses increased for decades following ACEs. Compared with adults without ACEs or those who have not experienced trauma in adulthood, individuals with ACEs (including sexual and physical abuse) are more likely to suffer from long-term PTSD and depression; simultaneously, they are more likely to take drugs, use more types of drugs, and have more serious drug dependence.

Thus, there is a clear link between ACEs and depression. Further, several researchers have found the comorbidity of depression and drug addiction; that is, depression may lead to drug addiction, and drug addiction can lead to or aggravate depression. Drug-addicted persons prefer to express themselves emotionally, and unpleasant stimulus may intensify their bad feelings and promote drug consumption. Avoidance of unpleasant effects is the major motivator for drug misuse.

Resilience is a dynamic process in which people may adaptively overcome stress and/or traumatic experiences (25). (25). It is the capacity to overcome life problems with endurance, self-awareness, and one's own internal coherence by activating a personal development project (26). (26). ACEs may create negative results, such as depression; nevertheless, some persons with ACEs may bounce back rather than suffer long-term negative repercussions, and they are thought to have superior resilience (27). (27).

It is useful to assist people to create and enhance resilience and to promote mental health education programs, which enable recovery from trauma and stress and lessen the effect of ACEs on depression.

In summary, there is a substantial association between ACEs and drug addiction. ACEs may induce and intensify depression, and sadness may be a key cause of drug misuse. Additionally, resilience appears to alter the link between ACEs, depression, and drug addiction. However, how ACEs impact drug addiction directly is far less explored, and the roles of resilience and depression in drug addiction are still unknown.

Therefore, this research first studied the association between ACEs and drug addiction and then analyzed resilience and sadness as possible causes of this relationship. To highlight the intricate link between ACEs, drug use, depression, and resilience more clearly

- Mental sickness.

Mental health concerns such as depression, post-traumatic stress disorder, and anxiety are all elements that lead to drug usage and addiction difficulties. People use drugs and alcohol to cope, but certain substances increase depression and anxiety.

People who have chronic pain issues might potentially develop hooked on opioids. Individuals frequently are administered this medicine after an illness, accident, or surgery to control a person's pain and recuperation. One difficulty with painkillers is that some individuals develop an addiction to them. A person without any of the risk factors might also become addicted at any moment. The longer someone is on a given painkiller, the tougher it gets to go off it.

The circumstances that lead to drug misuse are hard to overcome. But with the correct treatment and mentality, everyone who suffers from drug misuse and addiction may overcome their hurdles. If you or a loved one is battling addiction, do not be hesitant to seek treatment. Addiction is complicated but is also treatable. Get assistance today.

Chapter 4

HOW ADDICTION DEVELOPS

1)Avoiding coping skills and giving in to escape routes: Any person that constantly avoids addressing his/her issues would always resort to an escape route hence leading to addiction.

2)Neurochemical imbalance: Substance use disorders come from changes in the brain that might develop with chronic use of alcohol or drugs. The most severe form of the condition, addiction, is related to alterations in the function of brain circuits involved in pleasure (the reward system), learning, stress, decision-making, and self-control.

Every substance has slightly different effects on the brain, but all addictive drugs, including alcohol, opioids, and cocaine, produce a pleasurable surge of the neurotransmitter dopamine in a region of the brain called the basal ganglia; neurotransmitters are chemicals that transmit messages between nerve cells. This region is crucial for managing rewards and our capacity to learn depending on rewards. As drug usage rises, these circuits adjust. They cut down their sensitivity to dopamine, resulting in a decrease in a substance's potential to create pleasure or the "high" that comes from taking it. This is known as tolerance, and it represents the way that the brain maintains balance and adapts to a "new normal"—the regular presence of the drug. However, as a consequence, users typically increase the quantity of the drug they take so that they can obtain the degree of high they are accustomed to.

These same circuits govern our capacity to derive pleasure from everyday rewards like food, sex, and social connection, and when they are disturbed by drug use, the rest of life might seem less and less rewarding to the user when they are not taking the substance.

Repeated use of a substance "trains" the brain to correlate the rewarding high with other signals in the person's life, such as companions they drink or take drugs with, locations where they use substances, and accouterments that accompany substance-taking. As these signals become more connected with the drug, the individual may find it more and more difficult not to think about using, since so many things in life are reminders of the substance.

Changes to two additional brain regions, the expanded amygdala, and the prefrontal cortex help explain why ceasing usage may be so difficult for someone with a serious drug use problem. The extended amygdala governs our reactions to stress. If dopamine bursts in the reward circuitry in the basal ganglia are like a carrot that pulls the brain toward rewards, bursts of stress neurotransmitters in the extended amygdala are like a painful stick that urges the brain to leave unpleasant circumstances. Together, they control the spontaneous drives to seek pleasure and avoid pain and compel a person to action. In drug use disorders, however, the balance between these urges alters over time. Increasingly, individuals suffer mental or bodily anguish anytime they are not taking the chemical. This anguish, known as withdrawal, may become impossible to endure, prompting users to avoid it at any cost.

As a drug use disorder grows in severity, substance usage is the only thing that gives comfort from the negative sensations associated with withdrawal. And like a vicious cycle, comfort is acquired at the expense of a growing problem and higher anguish while not using. The individual no longer consumes the drug to "get high" but instead to prevent feeling down. Other objectives, including employment, family, and hobbies that formerly brought pleasure have problems competing with this cycle.

Healthy adults are usually able to control their impulses when necessary because these impulses are balanced by the judgment and decision-making circuits of the prefrontal cortex. Unfortunately, this prefrontal circuitry is also disturbed in drug use disorders. The outcome is a diminished capacity to manage the intense urges toward alcohol or drug use despite understanding that quitting is in the person's best long-term interest.

This explains why drug use disorders are believed to include reduced self-control. It is not a full loss of autonomy—addicted persons are still responsible for their actions—but they are considerably less able to overcome the overwhelming impulse to seek comfort from withdrawal given by alcohol or drugs. At every turn, people with addictions who try to quit find their resolve challenged. Even if they can resist drug or alcohol use for a while, at some point the constant craving triggered by the many cues in their life may erode their resolve, resulting in a return to substance use, or relapse.

LIST OF NEUROCHEMICALS.

- -Dopamine

- -Serotonin

- -Nonepinephrine/ epinephrine

- -Cortisol.

Chapter 5

STAGES OF ADDICTION

- Initiation:

This is the precise moment by which the addicted has been formally introduced to the substance(Drugs or persons) or behavior (Gambling, Game, Sex, etc) (Gambling, Game, Sex, etc.)

- Experimentation:

This is the stage the person attempts to participate in the usage of the drug or activity.

- Regular usage:

This point at when the drug or conduct is becoming an addiction.

- Risky usage:

When there's a missed of the material

- Dependence:

This is the point at which the person can not do without such a drug or activity.

- Addiction:

is the stage at which there is an inability to stop using a substance or engaging in a behavior even though it is causing psychological and physical harm.

Chapter 6

HOW TO KNOW IF YOU ARE ADDICTED

- Uncontrollably craving:

When there's an uncontrolled urge to become connected with a certain substance (eg drug) or conduct (eg sex) is a critical sign to recognize that you're hooked.

- Escape routes out of tension:

When you constantly hunt for an escape route out of stress is a sign that you're hooked.

- Decrease socialization

- Lack of interest in hobbies

- Ignoring negative repercussions

- Missing deadlines

- Taking danger to become a topic of Addiction.

Chapter 7

TREATMENT

- Refraining little by bit:

Total and instant abstention from any type of Addiction is highly harmful since it takes the brain time to acclimate to such circumstance and it require time to recover back to normal.

- SEEKING Counseling.